GOLDEN WEDDING ANNIVERSARY
Of
KEN AND PEGGY DYER

GOLDEN WEDDING ANNIVERSARY
Of
KEN AND PEGGY DYER

Half a century of being married, you make it to the Gold Standard. Gold represents the strength, wisdom, prosperity, and significance of your marriage. As a most prized metal, it is a symbol of the 50th wedding anniversary – something that cannot be replaced.

According to the National Center for Family and Marriage Research at Bowling Green State University, only 7 percent have reached the 50-year mark. You have beaten the odds of death and divorce.

Golden Wedding Anniversary of Ken and Peggy Dyer

ISBM: 9798356467653

Golden Wedding Anniversaries /2020 (For Time) and 2022 (For Eternity)
To our Posterity

Some Favorite Memories and a few of Life's Lesson's learned
By Grandpa Ken and Grandma Peggy

Introduction – "Getting Both Feet in the Boat".

On a wall in our Family Condominium in St. George, hangs a painting of the "Lion House", with the Spires of the "Salt Lake Temple" in the background. This picture tells the story of our marriage and the creation of our family.

On **December 16, 1970**, Ken and I were **married**, civilly (for our earth life), in the "Lion House". It was a cold winter night, in fact, the biggest snowstorm of the year. It was actually a very peaceful, quiet night, as only a few of our friends and family, dared brave the storm to attend our reception. I distinctly remember looking out the window at the heavy snowfall, and thinking how quiet the streets were, unlike most December nights in downtown Salt Lake, at Christmas time.

Later that evening when our reception ended, we had a long, slow drive to Provo. We were heading for Disneyland the next morning, so staying in Provo cut an hour off our drive the following morning. We were able to take this trip only because Ken's grandmother, Bethea Dyer, gave us **$100.00 for a wedding gift.**

Our first home, apartment, was located, in Sugarhouse, 1480 South 1100 East. It was a halfway point. Ken was in an accelerated program at BYU, getting his teaching certificate, and could not be employed. I was the sole breadwinner, the only time in our married life, and was working at Univac, the first computer company in Salt Lake. It was located by the airport, and we only had **ONE CAR**, so I carpooled with a couple of girls I worked with. As the "Proclamation" says, we were "adapting" for the time being. That was short lived. One year later we were living in Pocatello Idaho, where Ken was coaching, and teaching school. I was proudly a stay-at-home mom. The day we were to move out of our apartment in Salt Lake, to Idaho, **Brandon** decided to enter the world, five weeks early.

Our **first year of marriage**, while living in Sugarhouse, we attended our Sugarhouse Ward, only once. It was all elderly people. There were no primary, young men, or young women, so obviously there were no young families. We didn't feel comfortable there because we didn't have "**BOTH FEET IN THE BOAT**", so with a little encouragement, we jumped ship, and attended the Butler Ward, where Ken had lived, before we were married. We don't have the original letter, but actually had an official letter from the church giving us permission.

Lessons learned - Peggy – I was looking to be served and not to serve others therefore, "Getting Both Feet in the Boat" for me meant I needed to be more fully converted with my own testimony and personal relationship with Heavenly Father, the Savior, and the Holy Ghost:

Being born in the covenant to parents who were always active in the church, gave me, one foot in the boat. Growing up, as I listened to my parents pray each day, and my father read the scriptures to us, I knew, they knew God. I believed God and Jesus Christ existed, but I did not **know them personally.** To have a personal relationship, one needs to know how to effectively communicate, through prayer and scripture. We talk to God by praying. He always listens. He talks to us when we study the scriptures. The most important part of that conversation for me has been to learn how to recognize His voice, through the Holy Ghost. I eventually accomplished this through studying the scriptures, and words of the Living Prophets. While I was in high school and college, I took seminary and institute, but didn't understand enough to study on my own. I didn't know what questions to ask God, or how to find and recognize answers. It wasn't until I had seven children and took adult Institute that I began to figure this out.

Lessons Learned – Ken –"Getting Both Feet in the Boat" for Ken meant he needed to develop a HABIT of regular church attendance. That definitely happened as he later served in four different bishoprics, then served 6 years as a Bishop. He was a great Bishop and became known as the funeral, wedding, financial, and most important, "HOPE" Bishop. Whenever he counseled people, they always left feeling hopeful. He was called the funeral Bishop because he conducted 10 funerals. He performed 6 weddings including our own, Aaron and Alex.

Even though Ken was not raised attending church, it was evident the Lord's hand was in his life. He was raised by good parents and developed many great qualities growing up. His mother was LDS but inactive, and his father was a member of the Methodist faith until age 75 when Ken baptized him. While living in Soda Springs, next door to his grandmother, Ellen (Jones) Perkins, Ken got one foot in the boat as she took him to the LDS church until he was seven years old, then his family moved away. In Shelley, all of his friends were active members of the church and very good people, so he was baptized when he was eleven years old.

After high school Ken attended Ricks College with leader and athletic scholarships then graduated from BYU. Even though he didn't experience a full-time mission at that time, he was required to take institute while at Ricks and BYU. From those experiences, which he enjoyed very much, he gained a personal testimony, has a great memory of what he learned, and had a greater understanding of the gospel than I did when we met, even though I was grew up in the church.

Ken had to work on his **commitment** of regular church attendance because he grew up hunting and fishing with his father on Sunday. He warned me in the beginning, that because he had not been raised going to church every Sunday, I would have to be the one to get us there.

In August 1971, right after Brandon was born, we moved to **Pocatello**. Ken was teaching and coaching. We first stayed with Ken's parents in Shelley for a couple of months, while looking for an apartment to rent. We did not attend church while staying in Shelley but the apartment we found in Pocatello was right next to a church. Probably **not a coincidence,** because as I looked out my kitchen window at the church next door, I immediately felt a need to attend. On Sunday morning I got Brandon and myself ready to go. Ken was watching a ballgame on television and just remained at home. However, the following Sunday he joined us. The people in our ward immediately took us under their wing and Ken was soon on his way to becoming an Elder and we were on our way to the temple.

We lived in the Basement.

Pocatello 1971

A most important lesson: As soon as we began serious "**Temple Preparation**", Heavenly Father began pouring out blessings. He is always waiting to shower down His blessings, but He first has to wait on our choices, and use of agency. He knew we were going to have seven children, and that we could use an increase in salary. Ken was offered a job in Real Estate after one year of teaching and coaching. This also meant a move back to Utah, where we really wanted to live and raise our family.

On April 3, 1972, we were sealed in the Salt Lake Temple, and Brandon was sealed to us. This is why we love the painting by "Al Rounds" in our family Condominium of the Salt Lake Temple and Lion House because:

- It's "Our Story" and **a reminder** of where our life began and where we are now.
- It is also a reminder that as we did get "**Both feet in the Boat**". We now must endure, or "Stay in the Boat, and **keep progressing.**"
- This date, **April 3**, 1836, also has special meaning.   It was two days after the Kirkland Temple Dedication, the day **Elijah** returned to restore the **"Sealing Keys"**.
- Even more important it was the day the **Savior** appeared and accepted the Kirtland Temple and sacrifice of the people.

Bishop Andrus, in our **Murray ward**, gave us our first temple recommends. I remember him telling me he would give me a recommend on one condition, that I would use it regularly. It was very common at that time to only go back to the temple when you were attending a wedding. I have tried to keep that promise. By always paying an honest tithe, keeping a current temple recommend, and regularly attending the temple – Heavenly Father has kept His Promises to us and poured out many blessings to our family.

Almost exactly nine months after we were sealed, **Tiffany was born January 4, 1973.** In the next six years, **Travis, Brett, Brittany, and Marc** joined our family. **Symbolism** is the language of the Temple and, the number **SEVEN means COMPLETE.** We had a little space after Marc was born but five years later, in 1984, **Aaron** was born, and our family was COMPLETE. One of the greatest blessings for me was to be a stay-at-home mom with all our children.

Our Journey Through
the
"5 Stages of Marriage"

Laura Brotherson's
Book
"And They Were Not Ashamed"

My Marriage Relationship Journey
By Ken

One of my most important stories is my quest for a happy marriage. I must say it has been harder than I anticipated and also harder than it should have been. I am writing this in the 50th year of our marriage. It is now June of 2020, and we were married on December 16, 1970. I would like to share my experience with the hope that it may be of some help for present and future generations in preventing some of the mistakes I've made and also possibly a benefit in following a few good practices that I may have used.

In writing this I will use as an outline the "5 Phases of Marriage" as stated by Laura Brotherson, a wonderful marriage counselor that Peggy and I have both admired and also believed in her material as a handbook for our marriage and some of our children's marriages. We have never personally been counseled by her as a couple, but we have studied her material and teachings.

The five phases or stages of marriage for most people are: 1. Romantic stage. 2. Power struggle stage. 3. Awakening stage. 4. Transformation stage. 5. Real Love/Marital Oneness stage. I will attempt to tell, about my thoughts, feelings, and experiences as they relate to each one of these 5 stages in my marriage.

1. I feel that the "Romantic Love Stage" was particularly blissful in my perspective. We are attracted to that spouse that will make us whole by filling in the gaps of our personality. I was so naïve at this stage that I didn't know I had any gaps. I was just stunned by Peggy's beauty and her perfect smile to begin with. I became aware of the bonus of her sterling character and personal qualities in the first few years of our marriage. Our first child, Brandon, came soon into our marriage just as I was starting a new job coaching in Pocatello, Idaho. It didn't help that he was premature and had to stay in the hospital for almost 2 weeks while I was in Idaho and Peggy was staying in a camping trailer with her parents with no air conditioning while they were waiting to move into a new house. It was August, the hottest part of the summer and the only telephone was located in a shed outside the trailer. There was no such thing as a cordless or cell phone at that time!! She followed me to Idaho leaving her parents, friends, and everything else she was familiar with. What a stalwart! I never heard a complaint. We had almost no money, lived in a small apartment, no family or friends at first but it all seemed blissful to me. Maybe not so much for Peggy but if she wasn't blissful, she never told me. Looking back, I think it is the hard times when you are fighting to get ahead and find your niche in this world that really bonds you together as a couple. I am glad we had to go through that because we had a lot invested as our life got a little better and we had some successes together. I don't really remember when the power struggle stage began, probably when we became a little more financially secure. Maybe as couples we revert to that when we aren't worrying so much anymore if we are going to survive. So be careful!

2. We definitely got into the "Power Struggle Stage" and I don't like it and I don't like falling back into it from time to time. The recipe for avoiding this stage is found in the Book of Mormon in Alma chapter 7 verses 23 & 24 but most people don't seem to be able to follow it. My biggest problem I believe is my pride. I get too defensive if

someone points out my weaknesses. I am slow to learn that it is much better to be kind than right. Lest someone think that this is the story of our marriage, it isn't. Mostly it has been an awesome and satisfying experience for me in our marriage. I am grateful I can make a new start with our relationship when we stumble a little bit. I thank the Atonement for that and also a patient wife. A good and wise friend of ours once stated that a dis-functional marriage or family only happens when people stop trying. Most people that get divorced find out the same problems exist in the second or more marriages. A person is better off changing themselves instead of trying to change their spouse. It is curious that after you fix yourself, most of the problems disappear.

3. In Laura Brotherson's book, the "Awakening Stage" requires commitment, discipline, courage and a willingness to change by each partner. I also believe that it requires doing God's will instead of seeking after our own selfish desires that most often aren't good for us anyway. I think this is where Charity comes in, being more concerned about our spouse's happiness than even our own. That is not easy, and many people never get there. I wish I could say that I have finally achieved it but for me it has not been a destination, just still part of my journey. I will continue to fight each day for it because deep down I believe Peggy is worth it! During the time I served as a Bishop for 6 years in the Northridge Ward in Sandy, I compiled two help lists that would keep a person on the right path to achieve this awakening. I called them, "Tried and True Principles for a Happier Life and Marriage", and "Guidelines for a Lasting Marriage". I have included these lists in this section because following those guidelines and principles will certainly make a difference if a person can do them.

4. I feel I have partially obtained the "Transformation Stage" because I do not consider divorce as an option to a happier life. I'm pretty sure if I got myself transformed into the person the Lord wants me to be then I will also be the person that Peggy wants me to be. I have also heard that somehow Peggy will miraculously then turn into the person I want her to be.

5. I can't say I have permanently achieved the 5th and final stage of "Real Love and Oneness" yet, but I have had glimpses of it. I hope to really accomplish this stage before I die. Maybe because this stage is unnatural to mortals, I won't be perfect at it but I would like to be very consistent. The "Real Love Stage" has to be earned. There must be a continual outpouring of gratitude and joy. Unfortunately, I am too easily distracted and beset with worldly concerns. I will, however, get up tomorrow and try again.

TRIED AND TRUE PRINCIPLES FOR A HAPPIER LIFE AND MARRIAGE

1. Be grateful for even the smallest of blessings—a sunset, a flower, a smile – we are all beggars and unprofitable servants at the end of the day.
2. Be Wise Financially.
    a. Save part of your income every time.
    b. Avoid interest and debt.
    c. Save until you can pay cash for the wants in your life.
    d. Don't envy the things you can't or shouldn't have.
3. Be unselfish – be more concerned about the happiness and well-being of your spouse and children than you are about your own. Sacrifice brings forth the blessing of heaven.
4. Never, ever express criticism or negative comments to your spouse about them or their family. Let him who is without sin cast the first stone.
5. Never show anger or discord in front of the children, only love. The best thing a man (or woman) can do for his children is to love their mother (or father).
6. Build your spouses self-esteem and confidence with kindness and affection. Learn which of the five love languages are important to your spouse.
7. Make the Savior the focal point in your home. Be Christlike. As you become closer to the Savior, you will become closer to each other.
8. Continue to court each other. Make time for a date night each week. Take care of yourself and get enough exercise.
9. Don't be defeated by trials and tribulations. "For every adversity there lies the seed of an equal or greater benefit." What is the worst that can happen? Always have an eternal perspective.
10. Be happy! Be positive! It is a good life! Men are that they might have joy. Make each other the best you can be.

Ken Dyer

GUIDELINES FOR A LASTING MARRIAGE

1. Make the Lord a part of your marriage.
    a. Attend all your meetings.
    b. Hold a church calling and do service.
    c. Pay tithing.
    d. Read scriptures or Ensign and pray each day.
2. Nourish the friendship part of your marriage. Be best friends.
    a. Find and cultivate common interests.
    b. Make decisions together on finances, how to spend your time, etc.
3. Be balanced.
    a. Don't do anything in the extreme—too much T.V., too much time with friends, too much eating out, etc.
    b. Continue to grow spiritually, emotionally, and physically.
4. Be a hard worker and a smart worker.
    a. Be productive—avoid idleness.
    b. Do your work, before you play or rest.
    c. Think about your priorities.
    d. Do your best work every time—inspect your work to make sure it is good enough.
5. Be positive—avoid any negative thoughts, comments, or actions.
    a. Be happy and focus on the good things.
    b. It's difficult to change others—try to make yourself better.
6. Focus on those things which are eternal—family, relationships, the temple, and spirituality.
7. Be wise financially.
    a. Save part of your income every time.
    b. Avoid interest and debt.
    c. Save until you can pay cash for the wants in your life.
    d. Don't envy the things you can't or shouldn't have.
8. Be loyal.
    a. Trust and believe in your spouse.
    b. Forgive quickly and look for the best in each other.
    c. Be constant and faithful.
9. Stand in Holy Places.
    a. Avoid evil influences.
    b. Don't do anything that will limit your choices.
    c. Don't think about unrighteous things.
    d. Attend the Temple together and often.
10. Believe in yourself and in your potential.
    a. Don't be defeated when bad things happen.
    b. Assume the best will happen—don't worry about what negative things could happen.

Bishop Ken Dyer

Divine Priesthood Line of Authority Traced
PETER, JAMES and JOHN ordained Apostles by the Lord Jesus Christ (John 15-16).
JOSEPH SMSITH, JR. and OLIVER COWDERY
Received the Melchizedek Priesthood in 1829 under the hands of Peter, James and John.

The **THREE WITNESSES** to the Book of Mormon
(Oliver Cowdery, David Whitmer, Martin Harris)
were called by divine revelation to choose and ordain the **Twelve Apostles**.
On February 14, 1835 they were set apart for this purpose under the hands "blessed by the laying on of the hands" of the Presidency. Joseph Smith Jr., Sidney Rigdon and Frederick G. Williams.   (History of the Church, Vol. 2, pp. 187-188)

BRIGHAM YOUNG
Apostle February 14, 1835
By The Three Witnesses

JOSEPH F. SMITH
Apostle July 1, 1866
By Brigham Young

RICHARD R. LYMAN
Apostle April 7, 1918
By Joseph F. Smith

FRANK BRANCH MILLBURN
High Priest May 16, 1943
By Richard R. Lyman

GARY KENT MILLBURN
High Priest January 25, 1959
By Frank Branch Millburn

KENNETH MERLE DYER
Elder March 12, 1972
By Gary Kent Millburn

Gary Millburn, who ordained me an Elder, was the Elders Quorum President when we lived in Pocatello, Idaho.

September 24, 2004, Elder Ronald A. Rasband, who was our neighbor and in our ward, asked to Ordain me when I was called to serve as Bishop of the Northridge Ward.

Ken and Peggy Travels
By Ken

Oh, how we have been blessed to visit many countries and their people. Our purpose in traveling was to spend precious time together, broaden our horizons, and learn about the history and customs of other people. It isn't practical to elaborate on every trip. Peggy has made a list of all the places we have visited and the year we were there. We would like to tell about our favorite place and the things we saw and felt there. We both agree that place is Israel and Jerusalem. We have been there 3 times, the first in 1994 with Travis and the other 2 with Michael Wilcox and the "Fun For Less" Travel Group in 1997 and 2010. The first time we went with Thomas Travel and we didn't have a travel guide accompany us, which was pretty brave.

The travel agent told us that we could go stand on any corner in Old Jerusalem and be entertained for half a day. We found that to be true. Like they say, "different views for different Jews". I say that with respect, only used to describe all the different people we encountered with their robes, haircuts, prayers, hats, and customs. We floated in the Dead Sea with temperatures about 110', as I recall, we played on the beautiful beach in Tel Aviv, we took the tram at Masada to see where a thousand Israeli's held off a Roman Army on a mountain fortress for about a year before they all committed suicide rather than be captured.

We walked where Jesus walked throughout Jerusalem. We visited Golgatha (also known as Calvary) where Jesus was crucified, the Garden Tomb where He was buried, Bethlehem where he was born, the site of the last supper, the Sea of Galilee, Capernaum, and many other sites where He would have taught and healed. Special places where the Spirit and reverence were especially noticed were the Garden of Gethsemane, the Garden Tomb, and the Temple Mount where the Temple of Solomon was.

Of course, it isn't necessary to travel to Israel to feel the Savior's Spirit and influence, but we will be forever grateful that we have seen the special places that we read about where Jesus increased in wisdom and stature, and in favor with God and man. Luke 2:52 (One of Peggy's favorite scriptures).

One final side note is the tradition of purchasing some jewelry that is particular to the place that we have traveled. We have learned over the years that the value and beauty of the jewelry is long lasting and it will be a treasured memory of Peggy when it is passed on to daughters and granddaughters.

Grandpa Ken

Trips and Jewelry

During my school days, when I was young, I did not like learning or studying about History. My world was so small and simple I didn't see the need to know about anything outside my little world. Well about the year 1975 after 5 years of marriage and 3 children, Ken decided he wanted us to start traveling and take a trip once a year. His reasons for doing this were, he felt like it would be good for our relationship, and it would be fun to spend time with friends. We could now financially afford to go, and he wanted to do this while we were young and healthy rather than wait until our senior years. That was a good decision especially for me because now we are in our senior years I don't like flying or airports, so I am very grateful we did this while we were young. I am grateful for all the places and people I have been able to visit and learn about. There is a scripture - D&C 93:53 "It is my will that you should hasten to . . . . obtain a knowledge of history, and of countries, and of kingdoms, of laws of God and man, and all this for the salvation of Zion." This is a revelation that was given to the Prophet Joseph Smith in Kirtland in 1833. He talks about growing from grace to grace and about receiving a fullness of all truth. The glory of God is intelligence, and he wants us to seek after light, truth, and Knowledge.

In 1975 I was very reluctant to travel because I thought for sure my three little ones could not live without me for a week, but I soon found out that they not only survived but thrived. It was healthy for them and for me. It gave them special time with grandparents or friends and their little world expanded. Following is a list of all the many places we have been able to visit and learn about.

Year	Place
1976 – Feb 13-23	Hawaii
1977 Jan 22-30	Mexico City and Acapulco
1977 – June 26	Salmon River Trip
1978 – Mar 7-18	Sitmar Cruise
	Curacao, Caracas Venezuala, Grenada, Martinique, St. Thomas.
	Beginning Scuba Course – Coki Pt. Beach
	Virgin Island Diving Schools
	2 nights – Orlando - Disneyworld
1979 – Mar 18-29	Tahiti
	Moorea, Bora Bora,
1980 –Mar 13-25	Hawaii
	Kauai, Oahu Helicopter ride on Kauai
1983 –2/18-3/4	Tahiti
	Papeete, Huahine, Bora Bora, Raiatea, Moorea
1984 – Jan	Fiji

Jewelry – Black Pearl Necklace and Earrings

Marlo had an accident playing tennis and they left early.

1985 – Feb	Hawaii
1986 – 2/28-3/3	Mexico
	Cabo San Lucas, Mexico City, Zihuatanejo,

May 1986 - FOR MOTHER'S DAY KEN GAVE ME A GOLD, SILVER, AND COPPER
     NECKLANCE, BRACLET, AND EARINGS.

1993 – Nov	Tahiti	
	Went to Tahiti Temple and on an Ultra-light airplane	
1994 –8/30 – 9/10	Jerusalem,	Travis Ken and Peggy
	Thomas Travel – Jaffa, Cesarea, Tel Aviv, Dead Sea	

Jewelry – Widow's mite necklace

1995 – April	England and Scotland	
	London Temple, Lockwinnock, Kaim Home of the Orr's	
	Cemetery, Beith, Meikle Cloak	
1997 – June 6-22	Jerusalem with Michael Wilcox	
	Egypt - Cairo – Luxor, Tel Aviv, Galilee, Capernaum, Mount Tabor, Upper Galilee, Golan Heights, Jericho, Dead Sea, Masada, Bethlehem.	

Jewelry – Scarob Beetle Necklace and Lotus Flower Earrings

1999 – 2/27 -3/9	Brazil - Went to Visit Burgess's He was the Mission President Rio de Janeiro, Bela horizonte	

Jewelry – Amethyst and silver choker necklace with a large stone in the center. Amethyst necklaces for all the married girls.

Burgesses found a topaz stone that Ken purchased and had it set in a ring.

1999 – Aug 5-17	London Paris Theater Tour	
	Stonehenge, Althorpe, Buckingham Palace, Paris France, Visited **Andy Stephenson** on his mission – Louvre Museum Aston Rowant.	

2000 – May	Greece – Santorini	
	Tram – Cruise – Ancient city uncovered, Athens Acropolis. The Parthanon, New Corinth, Delphi, Arch of Constantine. ROME ITALY - Colosseum, Vatican City, Roman Forum, The Pantheon, FLORENCE ITALY.	

Jewelry – Gold Medalian with Ceasar Head. Gold/Silver chocker necklace shape symbol of Eternity with earrings.

2000 – June	New York City – Sacred Grove	Aaron
	Ken Ordained Aaron a Priest in the Sacred Grove.	
2001	Philippines and Hong Kong	Aaron
	Went to pick up Marc from his mission.	

Jewelry – White Pearl necklace and earrings.

2001 - Sept.	**Oklahoma City Temple**	
	Went to Temple with Phyllis	
2002	Hawaii	Travis and Jenn
2003	Ireland, Scotland	
2003 - Jan	Hawaii	Scott & Tiffany
2004	Hawaii	Aaron, Marc and Emily
2005 June 14-	Guatamala & Antiqua – Shelby Saberon	

Jewelry – Green stone with Silver – Necklace and earrings.

2005 Dec-Jan   Australia   Travis & Jenn
                    Fun For Less with Michael Wilcox   25ᵗʰ Wedding

2007   China – Fun For Less
Jewelry – Purple and gold necklace and earrings with Chinese symbol.

2008   Peru – Shelby Saboron and Wilcox's
Jewelry – Heavy silver choker chain with spikes coming out with tiny black stones – Necklace and earrings. Peru famous for silver.
Jewelry – Black stone in square center with silver necklace. With earrings.

2009 Dec.   Tahiti Cruise
Jewelry – Black Pearl on a chain

2009 Jan   New York – U.S. Open   Aaron and Alex

2010   Oberamergou, Germany, Switzerland & Italy.
                    Fun For Less Mike Wilcox

2010   Jerusalem/Egypt
Jewelry – 3 symbol braclet

2011   Australian Open   40ᵗʰ Wedding
Jewelry – Multi-colored small silver chain with Opal center and small earrings.

2011-2013   Mission to Philippines
Jewelry – Gold choker with two large brown and black pearls. Multicolered
        necklace with brown black white large pearls. Copper colored
        earrings and necklace we bought on the beach at Boracay.
            Large white earrings.

2013   Florida – Ell's Baptism
2014   Medeteranian Cruise
                    France, Monaco, Italy, Gibralter, Spain, Portugal
2017 - March   Hawaii - Brittany and Jeremy family
2017 - October   Normandy - Fred
2018 - March   Philippines DFG - Travis, Jen, Kylee, Oakley
2018 - Aug   Russia - Volga River Cruise and Moscow
2019 - April   Boston & Washington D.C. - Marc and Emily
Jewelry – Yellow Amber necklace and earrings
                    Alaska - Ken Fishing
Jewelry – Gold earrings with white stone – opal
                    Hawaii - Ken
Jewelry – All Gold necklace choker. $1,000.00 at time of purchase.
        (Probably 2 or $3,000.00 now.)

***Ken has always liked buying me jewelry, especially when we travel, so instead of buying souvenirs on our trips he bought me jewelry. It is something valuable that we can pass down to our daughters, and granddaughters, after we are gone.

Romance
The First Stage of Marriage - By Peggy

**President Gordon B. Hinckley said: "The most important decision of your life
. . . . . Marry the right person, in the right place by the right authority, at the right time."[1,2]**

Growing up in the church, I always thought I would marry a "Returned Missionary", in the Temple, right out of high school. Well, things didn't happen exactly in that ORDER or how I thought. But that was my GOAL, and it did happen.

My parents had no opportunity for formal education, so I didn't think I needed college. But, after high school when I had no prospects for marriage, I decided to follow my brother Fred to Dixie College, and look for a husband. As I was looking for my "returned missionary", I discovered it was important not to confuse the **culture of the church[3]** with the **standards**. I dated a few "RM'S" and became a little disillusioned and confused. One "RM", that my mother thought I should marry, was very dishonest. (Of course, she didn't know he was dishonest). But as Wendy Watson Nelson said, things are not always as they appear."[4] I began to see I needed to look for MORE than the TITLE "RM" so, he was **NOT** the **"Right Person"**.

My second year at Dixie, I dated a football player from New Mexico. He was not a member of the church but very familiar with the **"standards"**, and very respectful, so I kept dating him. Well, the time came when he wanted a commitment and I couldn't commit, because he said he would not join the church just so we could get married. Fortunately, the school year ended. I went home for the summer, and my friend Terry Gardner talked me into going to the Church College of Hawaii the next year. Being far apart made that break-up easier, and obviously again, he was **NOT** the **"Right Person"**. Statistics say - only about one in seven nonmember spouses are converted and baptized into the church. [5]

Ken and I **first crossed paths - my first year at Dixie** - in 1966 - in the Dixie College Gymnasium. Ken played basketball for Ricks, and I cheered for Dixie. However, that night while our teams were competing, and we were out on the gym floor together, we didn't even notice each other. Obviously, it was **NOT** the **"Right Time"**. But figure this out? After the game, someone lined Ken up with a Dixie girl whose last name was "Alldredge". Maybe there was a mix-up??

Ken Dyer

I spent two years at Dixie, one semester at the Church College of Hawaii, then the following year, in 1970, while attending Weber State College I decided I better start taking school serious because maybe I was going to be an old maid. Of course, that was when I met Ken. Our **first date** was in February to a basketball game, no surprise!! Our problem, he was attending BYU, and that wasn't convenient, so it wasn't until summer, that we started dating steadily. Saturday May 9th Ken attended the Weber State Junior Prom with me. On Friday, May 29th, I attended his graduation at BYU then over Memorial Day weekend we went to Idaho with Gary and Linda Peterson, for opening day of fishing on the Blackfoot River, no surprise! We spent the first night at his home in Shelley, where he grew up, and then headed for the river, early the next morning and stayed in the Peterson's camping trailer.

In August, we were on our way to a friend's wedding reception and got in a car accident. Fortunately, no one was hurt, but Ken's corvette was totaled. A Polygamist boy hit us. He had no insurance, and Ken only had liability insurance. So, Ken used the money he received, for the car parts that could be salvaged, to buy **my wedding ring.** One evening as we returned home from a date, it was around midnight, so I don't know if it was September 30th or October 1st, but he gave me my ring. He said, "I have something for you in my car glove compartment – in exchange for the remains of my car".

Even though we had been dating steadily for a while, my surprised reaction, he misinterpreted, and the next night he came to ask for the ring back. He had been engaged once before and that relationship didn't work out. So, if this wasn't the **"Right Time" and the Right Person",** he was getting out fast. However, the next night, at the end of our date, he asked if I wanted to **PRAY** about our **DECISION,** to know if it was **"RIGHT"**. Of course I said yes so we walked out in my dark, quiet,

back yard, knelt down by the barn and prayed. I vividly remember the experience and especially the **FEELINGS** I had as Ken offered our **first prayer together.** It all seemed "**Right**". **My FEELINGS were my <u>SIGN,</u> I KNEW I was marrying the "Right Person.**

My Patriarchal Blessing says I have the **gift of discernment.** We have to work to develop spiritual gifts but at that time I believe I was able to discern between the "**culture**" and "**standards**". Ken had integrity, was very open and honest, and I felt I could trust him.

Laura M. Brotherson, an LDS marriage therapist, said; **<u>"There is a reason you choose your spouse. Their psychological and spiritual makeup fit with yours in such a way as to create a sense of wholeness".</u>** 6

1.Pres. Gordon B. Hinckley - "Life's Obligations", Ensign Feb. 1999.
2.Bruce R. McConkie - "The most important single thing that any Latter-day Saint ever does in this world is to marry the right person, in the right place, by the right authority."
3. Elder Richard G. Scott – "Removing Barriers to Happiness", Apr. 1998.
4. Wendy Watson (Nelson) CD, "Things Are Not Always As They Seem". 2002
5. Eternal Marriage Student Manual (Religion 234-35) Background Factors pg. 188
6. Laura M. Brotherson, CFLE "And They Were Not Ashamed". P. 272.

The Power Struggle - The 2nd Stage of Marriage
By Peggy

Marriage is a psychological journey to WHOLENESS. It leads us from romantic love, through the **power struggle**, awakening, transformation, and upward to real love and oneness". 1

Throughout our married life, Ken and I have discovered the **many differences** that brought us together in the beginning. We continue to work on coming together, to fill the gaps, which make us **whole** as individuals and **one** as a couple. This takes sacrifice and work. Paul said in 1 Cor. 11:11 "Only together can a man and a woman, fulfill the Lord's plan". There are couples who stay together and live in the same house but live a parallel marriage. They never have conflict, but they do not **GROW** **to become whole and one.** What are some **differences** that create struggle? Gender, different personalities,2 speak different love languages,3 raised in different homes or environments and developed attitudes and opinions from our families of origin. Also, a person's life experiences create different perspectives, opinions, and views. All these differences are where the "power struggles" come from, in marriage.

There is one area in marriage that doesn't work well to have differences. Because we are all children of God, and we are all spiritual beings from the pre-existence, the **foundation** of a marriage is spiritual. Therefore, whether active in a church or not, especially if there are children in a family, it is better if parent's religious beliefs are the same. Children need to hear gospel truths taught and testified of by both parents. That is the "Law of two or three witnesses".4 Parent's teachings are strengthened and more believable when both parents have the same spiritual beliefs.

The biggest difference and problem in our marriage has been communication. The communication power struggle for Ken and myself has been mostly because of our family backgrounds. Ken's family is very **honest and open,** so they **freely express all their thoughts and feelings.** That is one reason I married him - but - with that pattern I sometimes take offense and pride creeps in. My family was the total opposite and lived by the Thumper Rule, **"If you can't say somethin nice, don't say nothin at all".**

Both, of these communication **patterns,** have some problems. So, we've had to figure this out. It hasn't been easy, and we learned the truth is, "Most people don't know how to handle NEGATIVE EMOTIONS in a healthy way. Most people EXPRESS or REPRESS negative emotions and neither of these responses, work well. They both damage relationships".5

For example: Dr. John Gottman, a researcher, identifies **FOUR** dangerous **communication patterns** that put marriage at risk:
1. Criticism – Character assassination. Personally, attacking and blaming.
2. Contempt – Resentment. Takes criticism to another level.
3. Defensiveness – Most common. Jumps in to correct and starts an argument.
4. Stonewalling – Avoids conflict because it's uncomfortable but then blows up down the road.6

Ken says his communication pattern is "**defensiveness**".
My communication pattern is "**Stonewalling**".

When we first got married, Ken would sit me down and say, "we need to talk, and you need to tell me everything that is bothering you". I would tell him a small amount but save most of it for when I was pregnant, or on vacation, and then I would blow.

Besides to be extra tired during pregnancy, I learned it's normal to have mood swings, feel fearful, and be easily irritated. On our vacations, my "Social Anxiety" would kick in and set things off because I was just out of my comfort zone being around people. **The power struggle began when - my "conscious expectations COLLIDED with my unconscious expectations".1**

Things worked out and we usually made peace before going home.

Early in our marriage, with children, work, church callings, and other diversions, distractions, and emotional drains,1 we didn't make as much PROGRESS as we should have in our communication. But later, when we became more AWARE, we became more serious about working on having effective communication.

In our retirement years, we are still trying to **progress and prepare** for Eternal Life with Heavenly Father, so we have worked hard to gain more understanding on how to become **whole** as individuals and united or **one** in our marriage relationship.

LESSONS I LEARNED ABOUT - Achieving Effective Communication

In 1975, five years into our marriage and with three children, I started going to **BYU Education Week.** Each year I have taken mostly classes on marriage and family relations, with an emphasis on COMMUNICATION. At first, I thought I was going to CHANGE everyone else in my family but, I soon learned the only person I could CHANGE was myself. I recognized I needed help and I have quite a collection of books and notes from my years at Education Week. I continue to work at it because change isn't easy and takes time. I often refer, back to things I learned over the years and then add to it. I have a favorite little book from **1992** by **Lili De Hoyos Anderson** who suggests 3 things for a REPRESSOR, which category I fit into. She suggests **three** ways to cleanse or **expel** our hurt or anger, in order to heal. These three appropriate sources are:

1. **Find a trusted listener.** When feelings are accepted and **validated** with empathy, (not approved of or agreed with), then feelings can lessen in intensity and the problem solving can begin. In marriage, we should be each other's trusted listener.
2. **Write in a journal.** This is a temporary workbook, eventually to be ripped up or burned so it never hurts anyone. This is not for posterity.
3. **The greatest source of emotional support is God.** Prayer can help us release hurt and anger but learning to connect spiritually and find emotional support from God requires great effort and practice.5

Because I have a hard time with face-to-face confrontation and communication, I turn to God a lot. I started to communicate by writing letters to Ken, and as my children went through their teen years, I often wrote letters to them. In face-to-face conversations I get too emotional, I can't think clearly, and I usually say things I regret.

Being a good listener and trying to **understand** the other person's view - are things we can do to have effective communication. The word "conscious" means to be aware of and respond. When Ken and I became aware of our communication patterns, we consciously began to work on this. With Heavenly Father's help, we have made significant progress over the past 50 years.

Ken and I did not start our marriage **praying together** every night but - we discovered, **"Marriage really does take three"** and COMMUNICATION WITH GOD every night, together, has been a great source of help and has created more unity in our marriage. Also, when we have differences, conflict, or a power struggle, the first thing I think to do is ask Ken for a **Priesthood Blessing.** That quickly brings Heavenly Father and the Savior into our relationship so we can then effectively communicate, with the Holy Ghost as our guide. It's the triangle – "Marriage takes three"!! "The Lord **Jesus Christ is the focal point in a COVENANT MARRIAGE RELATIONSHIP.** The Savior is positioned at the **APEX** of this **triangle.** As couples individually and steadily "come unto Christ" and **strive** to be "perfected in Him," (Moro 10:32) the man and woman come closer together."6

Agency in Marriage

Another important ETERNAL PRINCIPLE to remember in our marriage journey to wholeness is, individual **AGENCY.** It is a necessary, part of the Plan of Salvation. In the churches "Gospel Principles" manual we are taught, "If we were forced to choose the right, we would not be able to show what we would choose for ourselves. We are happier doing things when we have made our own choices. Agency was a principal issue in the premarital council in Heaven and was one of the main causes of the conflict between the followers of Christ and the Followers of Satan". Agency requires that there be a choice. There are 4 elements of Agency: 1) Opposition, 2) Law, 3) Power to choose, 4) Knowledge of good and evil. The **CONSEQUENCES**, whether good or bad, follow a natural result. We are not free to choose the consequences.

1. **Laura M. Brotherson CFLE "And They Were Not Ashamed"**. P. 272-5, 170-75.
   **When Laura counsels couples, the first thing she does is have them read and identify their own and each other's "Love Language".3 The "Natural Man" in us wants to speak our own language so, it takes some awareness, study, and practice to think and speak our spouse's language.

2. **Dr. Taylor Hartman – "Color Code".** I love Taylors "Color Code", and "Color Your Future" books - that he published in the 1990's. It has helped me understand myself, Ken, and other members of my family better: "There are **four basic personality types**, each assigned to a color. There are four clearly defined **paths** you can choose to walk in life. Your choices include (from most worthwhile to most detrimental): 1) charactered, 2) healthy, 3) unhealthy, 4) pathological.

Charactered people accurately identify and develop the strengths of their core personalities. Furthermore, they stretch to embrace the strengths of other personalities in order to compensate for their innate limitations. Embracing the gifts (strengths) of other colors, charactered people evolve. The more gifts they adopt, the more charactered they become, and the high they sour in flights".

3. **Dr. Gary Chapman - "The Five Love Languages".**
4. **Law of two or three Witnesses** - 2 For. 13:1; Deut. 19:15; D&C 6:28; 127:6; 128:3
5. **Lili De Hoyos Anderson** - 1992 Education Week & Book **"Ways to Communicate".**
6. **Dr. John Gottman - "The Four Horsemen of the Apocalypse".**
7. **Elder David A. Bednar - "Marriage is Essential to His Eternal Plan"** - Ensign - June 2006

A good reminder for me that I don't want to stay in the "Power Struggle" stage of marriage, is to listen to the song by Michael Martin Murphey:

What's Forever For
I've been lookin' at people
And how they change with the times
And lately all I've been seeing' are people
Throwin' love away and losing their minds

Maybe it's me who's gone crazy
But I can't understand why
All these lovers keep hurting' each other
When love is so hard to come by

So, what's the glory in living?
Doesn't anybody ever stay together anymore?
And if love never lasts forever
Tell me what's forever for?

I've been listenin' to people
And they say love is the key
And it's not my way to let them lead me astray
It's only that I want to believe

I see love-hungry people
Tryin' their best to survive
While in their hands is a dying romance
And they're not even tryin' to keep it alive

So, what's the glory in living?
Doesn't anybody ever stay together anymore?
And if love need lasts forever
Tell me what's forever for?

Awakening – The 3ʳᵈ Stage of Marriage
By Peggy

"The despair experienced in the **power struggle** is intended to invoke a **humble surrender** . . . . . and the awakening fosters a new acceptance and reality of each other and an enlightened realization of **marriage as the means for personal growth**."[1] This is a hard stage. This is the **CROSSROAD** in marriage when we basically have three choices:

1. **Settle for a parallel marriage which is an emotional divorce** – This means to stay married, live in the same house, both do your own thing - with not much unity or personal growth.
2. **Physical Divorce – Start over**. Because it is personal growth that is needed at this point in marriage, couples generally have the same problems, if they move on, to another marriage relationship. If there are children - that usually creates additional problems. "There are some exceptions and sometimes divorce is necessary".[2]
3. **Build "A Conscious Marriage" – "This is a marriage created by becoming conscious of, and cooperating with, the fundamental drives of our unconscious mind.** However, we must feel **safe**, to be **healed**, and to become **whole**."[1]
   a. This requires mental, emotional, and spiritual - work and growth.

"The romantic and power struggle stages - are meant to be temporary. The power struggle begins when - conscious expectations COLLIDE with unconscious expectations".[1] Some see the power struggle as a sign they married the wrong person. But instead - it is usually a SURE SIGN we are with the RIGHT PERSON for maximum potential growth.

- **The unconscious mind is** a reservoir of feelings, thoughts, urges, and memories that are outside our **conscious awareness**. Most of the contents of the unconscious are **unacceptable or unpleasant**, such as feelings of pain, anxiety, or conflict. The unconscious mind **influences** our behavior and experiences, even though we are **not aware** of these underlying influences. The unconscious mind can include **repressed feelings, hidden memories, habits, thoughts, desires, and reactions.**

As I dug deep into my unconscious mind, I became aware of negative, underlying influences that I needed to HEAL from. I discovered that when I have **negative thoughts, feelings, and fears - I want to keep to myself.** And it causes me to dwell on the negative. That uses up energy I could use to do something positive. "We must learn to detect inaccurate and **unhealthy thinking patterns** and learn how to **REPLACE** them with more accurate, healthy ones. Learning to identify and value our **emotions**, especially when we are young, can help us use them constructively to become more like the Savior".[3]

Ken and I chose to strive for "a conscious marriage". It hasn't always been easy because I personally still need a lot of validating, empathy, and healing. Therefore, Ken is learning to be patient. In a **conscious marriage,** "couples take an active interest in acquiring **strengths and abilities** they are lacking, rather than relying on their partner to **FILL EVERY GAP** or make up for all they are missing.

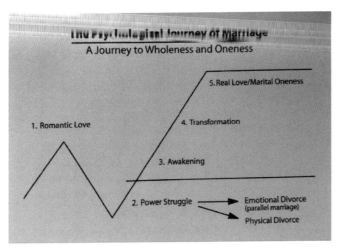

Where we once completed each other – in Stage One – we now need a desire to be WHOLE ourselves and one or united as a couple". 1

In stage 3 of marriage, "The Awakening", it is mostly **INDIVIDUAL** work.
In the **3 Dimensions of marriage**, ("The Triangle"), our spiritual path to the Savior is also INDIVIDUAL - but we can and must help and support each other in this process.4

Much of our unconscious anxiety can be from childhood. Those **memories and fears** can surface and affect us as adults and in marriage. This has been my experience. I know and am very aware that my unconscious anxiety, as a child and teen-ager, came from my sister, Bonnie's, handicap. This challenge was hard for my mother, and she never fully came to peace with it. I also struggled emotionally. I assumed from people's reactions, when we walked into a room, that EVERYONE was looking down on her and our whole family. People starred, laughed, looked away, and didn't' say anything. The word "Down Syndrome" didn't exist when I was young. "Down" was the last name of the man who figured out this particular mental illness was caused by a missing chromosome. In the 1940's to the 1960's "Downs" people were just labeled, "Mentally Retarded", or "Mongoloid". Most were institutionalized so, the general public was not aware of them, and shocked to see someone like that. I assumed people thought Bonnie was dumb and ugly and I not only felt bad for her but, I FEARED for myself, that I was also dumb, ugly, and would never get married, have children, and live a normal life.

- **With my family's communication pattern, we didn't openly talk about this much. The only thing I really understood was that Bonnie would be made WHOLE in the resurrection and be normal in the next life. My problem - that didn't help me in the moment. I also didn't understand I had PRIDE from the bottom looking up. Pride is a universal sin, also from the top looking down. Regular study in the Book of Mormon has helped me learn and remember the damaging effects of both kinds of pride. I learned, as I got older, that most people laughed, never said anything, and turned away, because they didn't know what to say or do. The truth is - "Down Syndrome" children are cute and funny. We laughed at, and with Bonnie, but it was out of love. It was somehow different if other's starred and laughed.**
- **Now that I'm older, I'm grateful for the experience because it is easy for me to have EMPATHY (feel what others feel) and talk to someone with a**

handicap, or their families. However, I still have to constantly be aware of my unconscious mind because I can still get offended easily.

As **Elder Holland** said, "Though we may **feel** we are 'like a broken vessel,' we must remember, that vessel is in the **hands** of the divine potter. **Broken minds** can be **healed** just the way broken bones and broken hearts are **healed** . . .

I bear witness of that day when loved ones whom we knew to have **disabilities** in mortality will stand before us glorified and grand, breathtakingly perfect in body and mind. What a thrilling moment that will be! I do not know whether we will be happier for ourselves that we have witnessed such a miracle or happier for them that they are fully perfect and finally 'free at last.'"4

I am grateful for Prophet's teachings and my parent's example of faith, hope and charity in their problems and marriage relationship. They didn't have a perfect marriage (there isn't such a thing). They didn't have marriage counselors nor all the psychological studies and help we have today. But they did have the spiritual dimension or gospel in their life. They also had their "Temple Covenants" that empowered them, protected them, and helped them work towards, and build, a Celestial marriage. I believe their **Spiritual Growth was key** to their enduring to the end. That is what the marriage triangle teaches us.

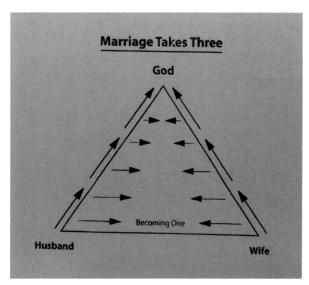

Marriage Takes Three

God

Becoming One

Husband   Wife

In the diagram "Marriage Takes Three": as husband and wife, each, draw nearer to God, they naturally draw nearer to each other until they become ONE at the Apex - where they also become ONE with God.   Elder Bednar **5**

Complete ONENESS is God's vision for Marriage.

Laura Brotherson teaches, "as **three-dimensional beings**", (body, mind, and spirit), - if we are to achieve a fulness of joy in marriage, **intimacy is also three-dimensional**. Spiritual, physical, and emotional. It's like a stool with three legs. If you take one leg away, it doesn't balance and will tip over). The emotional part has been difficult for me so I would like to share what I have learned. The emotional part of intimacy is a union of hearts.

• **Communication with empathy - feeling what someone feels (is better than compassion - just feeling sorry for them) increases emotional intimacy.** It is open and honest sharing of thoughts, feelings, fears, and joys.

• Emotional intimacy represents acceptance, friendship, love, trust, and feeling's of warmth and connectedness.

"• Connecting emotionally requires a willingness to be **vulnerable** and a profound sense of responsibility regarding each other's vulnerability."

"The Three Dimensions of Intimacy"

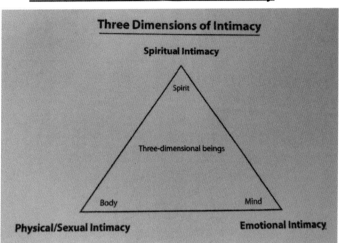

In a marriage relationship, we need to **feel SAFE sharing our inner self.** We need our companion to listen, show empathy, and especially **validate** that our pain is real. That doesn't mean we have to agree, but **"Validating is the first step in finding understanding and HEALING".**[1 & 3]

"The beginning of healing also requires childlike faith in the unalterable fact that Father in Heaven loves you and has supplied a way to heal. His son, Jesus Christ, laid down his life to provide that healing"[1]

Kay, Kim, Peggy, Fred
　　Jeanne, Suzanne, Bonnie, Fred
1964

1944 - Bonnie & Mom

- President Nelson says, "The sequence of Christs **pattern** that leads to His **healing power** is significant: **Faith, [daily] Repentance, Baptism [weekly sacrament], a Testimony and Enduring Conversion.** Conversion is turning from the ways of the world, and staying with, the ways of the Lord. Let us do small daily things that will give us spiritual strength. Then when converted, we can serve others, our family first which includes Temple and Family History work".6
- The spiritual habits I developed, have helped me **heal, feel peace, and create hope.** Elder Uchtdorf said: **"Because of Jesus Christ, our failures do not have to define us. They can refine us."**7

As I learned about the **AWAKENING** stage of marriage I thought about my children, grandchildren, and great grandchildren. My parents did their best. Ken and I tried to do our best in teaching and raising our children to be responsible adults. But our children and grandchildren have so much more information, to help them learn how to better deal with challenges and trials, to problem solve, and especially to understand all the **EMOTIONS** involved in life.

Church magazines are some of the best **resources** and are so accessible. The church is very in tune and up to date with all the current issues and challenges:

for example: The "Children's Friend", February 2018, had an article:

"Dealing with Strong Emotions".

As a child I needed help understanding my emotions, dealing with Bonnie. All children (and adults) need help identifying, understanding, and dealing with strong emotions. We must help children understand that difficult emotions are not wrong or bad. They are normal and can give clues to help us identify problems that need to be resolved. This article suggests dealing with a different emotion each month. It gives you **FOUR TALKING POINTS:**

1. Talk about what helps the child to feel calm
2. **Listen, empathize**, and let the child know they are heard.
3. Name the **feeling** and help the child **feel** safe.
4. Teach children correct behavior without punishing.

(I love the idea of the "**Indian Talking Stick**" - to help parents, children, and couples take turns learning WHEN to talk and WHEN to listen).

I learned about Indian ways when Phyllis Marquez, our "Indian Placement Sister" lived with my family for 7 years. (Her full story is in with my mother and father's life story.)

Transformation - The 4th Stage of Marriage
by Peggy

To **TRANSFORM** means to **CHANGE**. Elder Neal A. Maxwell stated,
"Transformation follows introspection".

"During the transformation stage of marriage, **new information and skills are gained, line upon line**, as difficult repairs, and healing occur. The awakening, and transformation involves a **purifying process of completely aligning ourselves with our divine spirit self and our will with God's will.** This is a heart-rending excavation of the soul that too few are willing to embark upon. Quiet reflection can help **make conscious the unconscious, so you can challenge and address feelings and beliefs."1 LB**

"Quietly reflect what you **think**—be **completely honest with yourself.** If you deny what you really **feel,** in order to give the correct answer, you will only be delaying growth you need, to attain fulfillment and marital happiness. **The Holy Ghost can teach you about yourself. The Spirit can help you become aware of incorrect beliefs you may have.** Also, you can **write** your thoughts and feelings. This will allow greater **access** to your **core beliefs and truest emotions** bypassing the culturally conditioned filter of the intellect".1 LB

I love this quote. It describes what I experienced as I tried to make conscious my unconscious. Transforming or changing oneself is not an easy process. I wish I had understood and started this process at a younger age. But, as I look back over my life, because I had the good guidance and influence of my parents, and because I was actively exposed to and involved in the church, I have been slowly gaining new information and skills throughout my life.

Following is a list of things I did to obtain new information and gain skills while I was young. Transformation starts young:

5. **Prayer** - The songs, "I am A Child of God", "Love is Spoken Here", "A Child's Prayer" and others - teach us while we are very young **WHO WE ARE** and **WHO HEAVENLY FATHER IS**. Learning about daily prayer, participating in it and

singing about it, was very important for me at a young age. I was raised by parents who helped me establish the simple, daily, kneeling, habit of prayer, at each meal and at bedtime. It's the small daily habits that transform us most.

6. <u>Keeping the Sabbath day holy, weekly partaking of the Sacrament, and quality family time</u> - This was how my family spent our Sunday's. The Savior transforms us through our covenants with Him at church. Then, we were usually always with extended family and established close family ties.

7. **<u>Baptism</u>** - Learning and applying the "**Doctrine of Christ**", began with my baptism, July 4, 1956. My father baptized and confirmed me, then with both parent's help, I progressed along the **covenant path** learning how to build my faith, how to repent, and how to **RECEIVE guidance from the Holy Ghost.** In that process, **I began to build a personal relationship with My Father in Heaven and His son Jesus Christ**. By still renewing my covenants weekly, this keeps me on the path.

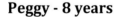

Peggy - 8 years   **Peggy, Fred - back row**
                             Kim, Kay, Suzanne - front row

Pres. Nelson made **three important statements** about **transformation**:

4. "Daily repentance is a process of changing our heart. It is allowing the Savior to **TRANSFORM US.**"2

5. "The new home-centered, Church supported curriculum, if followed through conscientiously, has the potential to **TRANSFORM our HOMES** into a sanctuary of faith".

6. "I urge you to find a way to **make an appointment regularly with the Lord—to be in His holy house**—then keep that appointment with exactness and joy. **I promise** you the Lord will bring the **MIRACLES** that He knows you need, as you make **sacrifices** to serve and worship in His Temples."3

6. **Piano Lessons** - Transformation is like learning the piano, which I did during my growing up years. It took DAILY PRACTICE. Developing a talent is a cumulative PROCESS - so it is hard to see the daily PROGRESS.

One of the greatest benefits from learning the piano was my exposure to good music. **Listening to uplifting and inspirational music daily** invites the spirit quickly into our **mind and heart**, especially primary songs, and hymns. I often have this kind of music playing in my kitchen as I am working. Any time I feel a need to **TRANSFORM** a negative thought or feeling, (into clearer thinking and a peaceful feeling),

I turn on the song:

Where Love is—There God is also, Where God is we want to Be.

5. **Education** - created a **huge Transformation for me** -

Secular and religious are both important and need to be balanced.

When I was in Jr. high and high school if there was anything difficult or that I didn't understand in my classes, I feared asking the teacher a question because I didn't want anyone to think I was dumb. Consequently, I didn't obtain all the new information or develop the skills I could have at that time. but I did graduate from High School!!!

Seminary was a good experience, and I always had a good feeling there. I'm know my faith and testimony of the gospel grew from those classes and teachers.

Going back to school at BYU, when I was 60 years old, and getting my **Bachelor's Degree in "Family Life"** was, a very important experience for me for several reasons:

2.   Raising 7 children I realized I needed all the education I could get. In the beginning I thought being a stay-at-home-mom would be an easy job. WRONG!

3.   After reading Maria Hafen's Book, "Celebrating Womanhood". She explains that women need to experience both education and motherhood, if possible. It isn't about choosing one or the other.

4. Learning how family's function, not just my own little family but also extended family, was especially important for me. The family realm can be the best of human life and the worst of human life. The best parts are experienced as we find deep joy and the greatest pleasure from our interaction with those who we love and love us. Family life is a crucible that refines, tests, and helps us grow and mature in ways that are noble, great, and wonderful. If we are wise in the way we manage this precious part of our lives, family life can provide satisfaction, fulfillment, love, security, a sense of belonging, and other beauties and riches that are difficult to attain outside the family realm.

5. I wanted to send a message to my daughter's, granddaughter's and great granddaughter's - that Education is very important and Lifelong-learning should be everyone's goal. That's why I love yearly "BYU Education Week".

e. One of my favorite, and most helpful classes at BYU was - **"As a Man Thinketh"** (Proverbs 23:7).   The teacher gave us the following **questions to memorize,** and challenge, any negative thoughts. Our thoughts change or transform us for better or for worse.

- **Rules for Rational Thinking**
- Is my thought based upon objective reality (as opposed to subjective or personal opinion)?
- Does thinking this thought help me protect my life, health, and well-being?
- Does thinking this thought help me achieve my short or long-range goals?
- Does thinking this thought help me avoid or prevent conflict with others or within myself.
- Does thinking this thought help me feel the way I prefer to feel".

A group of hymns and talks that reminds us to "Let virtue garnish [our] thoughts unceasingly" is (D&C 121:45-46) and Elder Ulisses Soares, (October 2020) He said, **"Seeking Christ in every thought and following Him with all our heart requires that we align our mind, and the desires (of our heart) with His.** By focusing daily on the Savior, we may achieve 'The Peace of God which passeth all understanding."

Ken graduated from BYU in 1970 and I graduated in 2009.

6. **Accepting Church Callings** – (**Service -transforms us,** as it gets us out of our comfort zone, and away from obsessing over our own problems or goals.) -

My first church calling was in high school.   I was called to be the Sacrament Meeting Organist. Since we have been married Ken and I have both always had opportunities to serve through our church callings. Visiting teaching, home teaching, and ministering - being some of the most important service we have done.

Trek with Brittany   Girls Camp   Trek with Bishop Dyer

I spent a lot of years in the Young Women's organization

In 2019 the church came out with a new program for the children and youth to help with their personal development. This **pattern for growth** can help all of us develop in the four same areas that Jesus did. **Luke 2:52** says **"Jesus increased in wisdom, and stature, and in favor with God and man."**

I first discovered this scripture, teaching young women in 1978. I loved it then and have tried to apply it for a long time. This is the perfect scripture to help us become **personally WHOLE, and one in our marriage relationships.** With the right kind of knowledge, and help through our **Patriarchal Blessing,** we can work to become balanced like the Savior, mentally, physically, spiritually, and socially.

7. **Following the Prophets, apostles, and teachings in the scriptures is one of the best ways to obtain new information.** With all my insecurities as a youth, I very much depended on the arm of flesh. I was like the people in **John 12:43 - "They loved the praise of men MORE than the praise of God".** I went to work on my **outward appearance**—hair, make-up, clothes, friends, etc.—so I would be **accepted.** I wanted to feel like I **belonged**.

<u>The Bus Stop</u>

When I was 65 years old, I ran into a cousin, Duane Olson, who I had not seen since high school. As we were talking, he said, **"Do you know what I remember about you?"** I had no idea what he was going to say. Then he said, "You would roll up your skirt every morning when you got to the bus stop!".

When I was in high school, we were not allowed to wear pants. We wore dresses or skirts every single day. During those years, the fad or style **changed** from wearing skirts, below the knee, to above the knee. My mother would NOT allow me to shorten my skirts so, I just rolled them up a notch when I got to the bus stop every morning. **Be careful what you do because you never know who is watching and what they will still REMEMBER - 48 years later!!!**

In 1970, when Ken and I were endowed and sealed in the **Salt Lake Temple,** skirts had gotten even shorter. I must have ignored the counsel given in the temple, about how to wear my temple garments. But this time instead of rolling my skirt up, I must have **rolled my garments up.** My dresses would NOT have covered them, especially when I sat down. I am grateful Heavenly Father is patient and waited for me to MATURE and TRANSFORM my attitude.

Ted J. Freeman, one of my very favorite teachers at BYU Education Week wrote a book, "The Temple - Gaining Knowledge and Power in the House of the Lord". He uses **TWO WORDS** to help us understand the **SYMBOLISM** of temple garments. These two words - **GARMENTS** and **NAKED OR NAKEDNESS.**

"**The prophet Jacob** indicates that **TWO GROUPS** are involved in this concept at the DAY OF JUDGEMENT:

5. The "NAKED" - will have a perfect knowledge of all guilt, uncleanness, and nakedness.

6. The "CLOTHED" - will have a perfect knowledge of their enjoyment, being clothed with purity, or the ROBE OF RIGHTEOUSNESS. (2 Nephi 9:14)"

"**The Prophet Joseph Smith** prayed at the dedication of the Kirtland Temple: "That our garments may be pure, that we may be clothed upon with robes of righteousness. Through studying the symbolism and scriptures related to the garment, we come to see that the garment symbolizes both coats of skin and robes of righteousness. They are a **PROTECTION** against temptation and evil and a **REMINDER** of the covenants we make in the temple. Our garments may be cleansed in the Lord's blood, through the enabling power of the Atonement, and we are to wear them when we meet the Lord.

I discovered, after a serious study of the scriptures, the answer to all my insecurities, as a teen and adult, was to work on my **inner spiritual** self, my faith, and my relationship with God. When I do this daily, I receive peace and confidence through the spirit.

Well, here I am, 50 years later and I love wearing my temple garments, [the way they are meant to be worn - not defiling them - or violating the covenants and promises I made with God.] I hold sacred my covenants because, I want the physical, and even more important the **spiritual PROTECTION and power to overcome the temptations of the adversary**. I am grateful for and have memorized the symbolism or meaning of the four simple embroidered marks on my temple garments that serve as a daily, constant **reminder, of my relationship with my Savior.** I now more fully understand and love wearing my temple garments.

Transforming Fear to Faith has been my life challenge. My growth has been in baby steps. It started as a child, continues today, and will be a lifelong process. Now that I am 74 years old, recently diagnosed with **"Pancreatic Cancer"**, and have NO HAIR, I am not worrying about what others think. I daily rely on the **WORD OF GOD** to transform - my Fears - into FAITH in my Savior Jesus Christ, and that gives me HOPE in his many promises that I can become what I need to be, to return and live in the presence of my Father-in-Heaven. It also gives me PEACE in this life, as I just received the results of my CT test SCAN, after 5 rounds of Chemotherapy, and I know I have been **blessed**. I believe answers to many prayers have been heard and I have been blessed with more time here on earth as my tumor has shrunk by 1/3 and there are no new tumors growing. My doctor said he has only had 20-30% of his patients have that kind of success.

Becoming a Wife, and Mother of Seven Children, has been my biggest Transformation and my greatest blessing!!

Within the first year of our marriage, Ken and I had several BIG CHANGES or transformations!!! Brandon was born, Ken got a coaching and teaching job in Pocatello, Idaho, so obviously we had to move. I remember vividly, Thursday, August 12, 1971. (My water had broken, five days earlier as I was sitting in the grandstand watching Ken play softball. I called the doctor and he said he wanted me flat in bed because I was six weeks away from my due date). The day Brandon decided to be born, I was not in bed, because we were supposed to be moved out of our apartment in Salt Lake and Ken was supposed to be in Pocatello to start his new job.

Soon after Brandon was born, Ken left for Idaho and Brandon had to stay in the hospital, because he was premature. My parent's were building a new home and temporarily staying in their camping trailer, in the middle of a dirt field. There was no such thing as a cell phone. The closest phone was in a shed outside the trailer. It was hot, there was no air conditioning, and that was my home for now. I shed a lot of tears because I had no husband, no baby, and no home. What I did have, that saved me, was a good friend, Mary Ann Hyatt, Andreson, who came to visit me and console me.

There have been many, different kinds of changes throughout our life. That first year in **Pocatello** was just the beginning. Change makes life exciting with new opportunities. We met lots of great people along the way, that have changed our lives for the better. In our first five years of marriage, we lived in five different places.

Following a list of HABITS Ken and I incorporate throughout our 50 years of marriage, to help us learn new information, obtain skills, and to help create a "Conscious Marriage".

Daily

1. **Follow the Living Prophets and Apostles** - Study the General Conference talks and read the monthly Ensign (Liahona).   3 Nephi 19 tells us - **IF** we **believe** the word of God, which they speak, our faith and hope in Jesus Christ will increase. They help us understand and apply the scriptures, and they help us **progress** along the covenant path:

Living Prophets during our Lifetime

The Prophet and President when Ken and I were born was - <u>George Albert Smith</u> – 1945-1951. (8th President of the Church)

- 9th President <u>**David O. McKay**</u> 1951-1970 – The prophet Ken and I remember most because he was President all through our childhood, teenage, and young adult years.   This photo is when I was at Dixie College. The Homecoming Royalty was invited to go to Salt Lake and meet with the Prophet in his home.
- Wow!!! What a privilege!!!!

- 10th President **Joseph Fielding Smith** Jan. 1970- July 1972 – The prophet when we were married, when Brandon was born, and when we were Sealed in the Salt Lake Temple. I love his quote about the Holy Ghost. **"The Spirit of God speaking to the spirit of man has power to impart truth with greater effect and understanding than the truth can be imparted by personal contact even with heavenly beings. Through the Holy Ghost the truth is woven into the very fiber and sinews of the body so that it cannot be forgotten."**
- 11th President **Spencer W. Kimball** 1973-1985 - Tiffany, Travis, Brett, Brittany, Marc and Aaron were all born during this time.
- 12th President **Ezra Taft Benson** 1985-1994 – I was born in the church or in the covenant, but this was the Prophet when I became **fully converted** with my own testimony. These were the years I really focused in by listening to and reading and studying all of the conference talks. Pres. Benson's focus was on the Book of Mormon and Pride.
- 13th President **Howard W. Hunter** 1994-1995. Focus was the Temple.
- 14th President **Gordon B. Hinckley** 1995-2000. Building more small temples.
- 15th President **Thomas S. Monson** 2008-2018 Book of Mormon and Temple.
- 16th President **Russell M. Nelson** Jan. 14, 2018-   "The Gathering".

2. **Read scriptures alone and together** - I wasn't good at reading scriptures when I was young, but my father set a good example as he loved and read his scriptures daily. Ken and I started reading on our own, regularly, after we moved to Granite. It was about 1990 when we started having family scripture with the children. On our mission, we developed the habit of daily couple scripture study. My favorite scripture study is: 1. One Conference Talk a day and 2. learn the meaning of one new word a day using information from the Topical guide and Dictionary.

PATRIARCHAL BLESSINGS - OUR PERSONAL SCRIPTURE
I received my **Patriarchal Blessing** when I was 17 years old. I was just starting my Senior year in high school. At that time, I didn't really understand the importance of it and didn't read it much. As I got older and learned the benefits of reading and studying it often. As my children reached their teen-age year's I encouraged them to read their blessings often. I love reading my children, and grandchild's Patriarchal Blessings. It helps me see them through Heavenly Father's eyes and I can better parent them as I encourage and remind them to go to their blessing when they have questions or struggles.

January 4, 1976, after Ken and I were married, had 3 children, and were living in our first home in Granite, Ken received his Patriarch Blessing. Patriarch Thomas Ward asked him, "Do you think this is the first time you have had this blessing?" He said, "You don't think Heavenly Father would send you to earth, without a Father's blessing, do you? I am just RESTORING the blessing He gave you."

God gives us knowledge line upon line as we study His word daily. **A Patriarchal Blessing is our own personal scripture.** I believe Patriarchal Blessings are evidence God knows, loves, and is very aware and interested in each of us individually.

Weekly
3. **Family Home Evening and Come Follow Me** This is an important time for family communication, bonding, learning, and practicing gospel principles.

We have a lot of great memories of time together as a family.   And I believe they are still close and enjoy being together, now that they are all older and married, because of those bonds that were created when they were young.

4. **Adult Institute classes** - I started in 1990, at our Stake Center. I attended Michael Wilcox classes for 16 years and Ken came with me the last 8 years. We also traveled with "Fun for Less" with Michael as the Educator. A benefit of COVID is, now the institute classes are all on "Podcasts" so you can listen to whoever we want, anytime, anywhere. (Photo with Mike and Laurie Wilcox in Peru - March 2008)

Hiking - Machu Picchu

5. **Weekly DATE NIGHT**. Ken was the one that made this happen in our relationship. It's important to keep this relationship strong because very quickly the kids are gone and have their own lives to live.

6   ~~Fast pray with a purpose, and pay a generous fast offering~~   We took full
responsibility for this obligation - to give to the poor and needy. He gave very generously.
However, he called it **SLOW DAY, instead of fast day** because the day seemed very long,
when he had to go without food.   One Sunday I had a meeting after church and when I
finally got home Ken and all the kids were laying on the floor, each with a sign over their
body that read:

DEAD FROM STARVATION!!

7. **Pay a full tithing** - Ken became fully committed to this commandment when we first
went to the temple to be sealed. I am grateful he took on this responsibility for us because
he has never missed paying it. Tithing is about putting **God First** in our lives.

Michale Wilcox says: "Our ATTITUDE toward TITHING and our TEMPLE
COVENANTS must be serious. Young people often go to the temple with the desire only to
get married, without realizing the **obligations** they take upon themselves. Tithing is often
the major obstacle that keeps them from RETURNING OFTEN to RENEW and keep those
covenants". (S. Michael Wilcox - "House of Glory".)

Tithing is a "principle with a promise". Ken and I have had our lives blessed
abundantly, especially in having the HOLY GHOST abide with us as a guide in our marriage
and within our family.

To Teach the Children about tithing:
Watch - "The Widow's Mite: A Bible Story for Children - You Tube

Yearly

8. **Education week** (Peggy) for 42 years – This tradition originated with my
mother. I started attending with friends in 1976 and only missed it while on our
mission. Our married children started attending with me after they had children.

Brittany babysitting Lexi

9. **Family History work.**
We started this in 1978
after Ken received his
Patriarchal Blessing. He
felt prompted to do work
for his Ancestors because
it says he would
be a Savior to his family.
This means he would
need to **sacrifice** to do it.

Our children and Grandchildren have helped do many Baptisms and Confirmations.

10. **Missionary work.** We served an 18-month full-time mission to the Philippines in 2011-2013. We should continue to look for opportunities on a daily basis.

11. **A yearly VACATION** - A get away together as a couple. Even if it was to St. George or somewhere close. Ken was the one that made this happen.

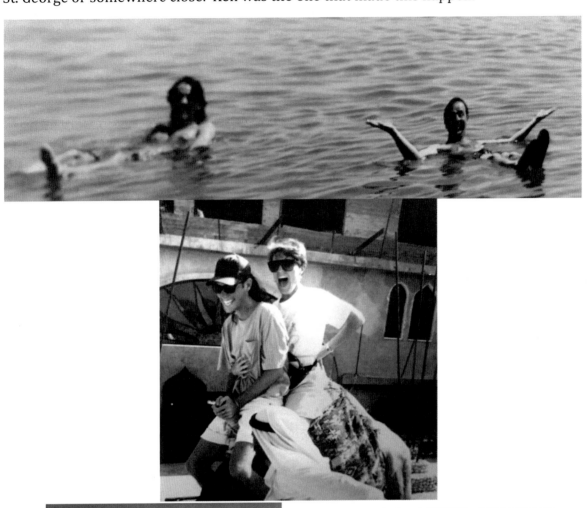

This may seem like a long list but we have had 52 years to experiment, gradually accumulate, and incorporate these **habits**. (Ken has two lists he compiled while serving as a Bishop.) These things have helped us heal, feel peace, and create hope in our marriage relationship and family. These **habits** have especially helped us come to know and trust the Savior and they continue to help us endure to the end. As we keep working on becoming whole as individuals, and one or united as a couple, our desires become more like the Saviors. **Our biggest help throughout our 52 years of marriage has been to learn to RECOGNIZE and FOLLOW the individual promptings that come from the companionship of the HOLY GHOST.**

After becoming **CONSCIOUSLY** aware of the word **TRANSFORMATION** or change, I can't believe how often I see it used. Especially with leaders and teachers in the church. Emily Belle Freeman in her book, "**Grace to Become**" said:

"God's plan for each of His children includes progress, increase, and TRANSFORMATION. At the center of that plan is Jesus Christ, who offers enabling grace through His Atonement. This enabling strength includes - SAVING GRACE, which helps us OVERCOME, and EXALTING GRACE, which helps us to BECOME."

Real Love/Oneness - The 5th Stage of Marriage

By Peggy

"Dr. Harville Hendrix contends, **Real Love lasts. It is built upon** the rock of **CHARACTER CHANGE**, which makes it possible to **hold the experience and maintain it when the STORMS come**".1

Remember in "Stage 1 of marriage, virtues were magnified during courtship. Weaknesses that seemed small during courtship grow to sizable proportions after marriage. Married couples need to read each other's Patriarchal Blessings, especially when there are struggles. This helps to remember our **spouse's strengths,** the things they do well, and why we married them. We need to be AWARE of each other's **weaknesses** - but focus on their **potential.**

"Weakness is not Sin"

Weakness CAN lead us toward Jesus Christ. As couples, **IF** our weaknesses turn us to God, together we develop humility, patience, long suffering, gentleness, and kindness. **We can change ourselves, support each other,** and pray for each other. In traveling with Michael Wilcox, visiting other countries and learning about other religions and people he said, "never judge others by their worst. Instead, focus on what they do best". That's good marriage advice.

One of my weaknesses, my Patriarchal Blessing mentions is - "Overcome my timidity and be unselfish in bearing my testimony". This means openly "COMMUNICATE" my thoughts and feelings. This means overcome my "Fears" and replace them with "Faith".

It's not one experience, or church calling, that diminished my fear and increased my faith. It has been a gradual process that I attribute to all of my church callings. I still have fears, one of which is public speaking, but I am grateful, for what I learn in my study and preparation. I appreciate the opportunity to bear testimony of the truthfulness of the Gospel, and to give credit to Heavenly Father for everything in my life. "Faith" is something that has to be maintained daily - through prayer, scripture and service. It still takes effort for me to stretch out of my comfort zone.

Elder Neal A. Maxwell observed: "It is not an easy thing . . .to be shown one's weaknesses . . .Nevertheless, this is part of coming unto Christ, and it is a vital, painful, part of God's plan of happiness. In **Ether 12:23-27 we are told God gives men weakness. If we come unto Him, He will show it to us.**

As I have tried to overcome my timidity - I know the most important people I need to 'be unselfish with in bearing my testimony' are - my husband, my children, and grandchildren. I am grateful for the **example of my father** who bore his testimony often - with conviction - both at church and at home. **Conviction arose in my heart, each time I heard my father bear his testimony. His strength and example helped me overcome my timidity.**

Strengths

Patriarchal Blessings can also reveal our spiritual gifts or strengths. President Oaks gave a talk entitled, **"Our Strengths Can Become our Downfall."** (BYU Fireside June 7, 1992) He said Satan will attempt to cause our spiritual downfall through tempting us to misapply our spiritual gifts. The scriptures tell us there are many gifts and every man is given a gift of the Spirit of God. These gifts come from God and are to be used for the benefit of all of God's children not just for ourselves.

I spent much of my life being a very **DEPENDENT** person. I thought being dependent on the Lord was a good thing and a STRENGTH. However, after I read President Oaks talk, I learned this needs to be balanced. "A desire to be led by the Lord is a strength, but it needs to be accompanied by an understanding that Heavenly Father leaves many decisions for our personal choices.

<u>**We should study things out in our mind, using the reasoning powers our Creator has placed within us. Then pray for guidance and act upon it if we receive it. If we do not receive guidance, we should act upon our best judgment. Revelation from God is a sacred reality, but like other sacred things, it must be cherished and used properly so that a great strength does not become a disabling weakness."6**</u>

As I have studied our Patriarchal Blessing's I learned Ken and I have the same spiritual gift, the "**SPIRIT OF DISCERNMENT**" to enable us to **UNDERSTAND THE HEARTS and NEEDS of those with whom we associate."**

A spiritual gift I greatly desire is to be, "MEEK AND LOWLY OF HEART". Elder Bednar in April 2018 said, "MEEKNESS IS NOT WEAKNESS. IT IS A DEFINING ATTRIBUTE OF THE REDEEMER AND IS DISTINGUISHED BY:

1. RIGHTEOUS RESPONSIVENESS,
2. WILLING SUBMISSIVENESS, AND
3. STRONG SELF-RESTRAINT.

I have tried to remember and practice these **RESPONSES.**

Patriarchal blessings often warn of Satan. His plan is NO AGENCY. He knows and uses our strengths or weaknesses to rob us of our agency and potential and make us believe we are not capable of keeping God's commandments or doing what Heavenly Father has sent us to earth to do. The only way to truly reach our full potential, and help others is, yoke ourselves to the Savior. FAITH is mentioned seven times in my Patriarchal Blessing. We are taught in the scriptures, (Moroni 7:33, 40-48), that **FAITH, HOPE, AND CHARITY** are the **FIRST** gifts we must seek, ask for, and work to develop, before we can move on to developing other spiritual gifts.

INTERDEPENDENCE in Marriage

Well as I spent most of my younger years being too **DEPENDENT**, when I got older, I started becoming too **INDEPENDENT.** "By valuing differences, we become interdependent and create cooperation". As we complement and complete each other in marriage, we become one and united.

EQUAL PARTNERS in Marriage

"In an equal-partner marriage, both bring a **spiritual maturity,** both have a **conscience** and the **Holy Ghost** to guide them. Both see family life as their most important work. Each strives to become a fully rounded disciple of Christ—**a complete spiritual being**. In an equal-partnership, love is not possession but participation which **merges into the synergistic eternal ONENESS."**

"In the little kingdom of a family, each spouse freely gives something the other does not have and without which neither can be complete and, return to God's presence.

- **Spouses are not a soloist with an accompanist, nor are they two solos. They are the interdependent parts of a duet, singing together in harmony at a level where no solo can go."**

When I walk ALONE, I take something uplifting to memorize and focus my thoughts on. My favorites are "The Family Proclamation" and "The Living Christ".

In the Proclamation it tells us that after Adam and Eve were married in the Garden of Eden, the "**FIRST COMMANDMENT**" God gave was to "**MULTIPLY AND REPLENISH THE EARTH**". Ken and I kept that first commandment and I'm sooo grateful for our children. They came **early** in our marriage. Brandon was born during our first year of marriage. In our first 8 years of marriage, we had six of our seven children. We didn't really plan things that way but, I couldn't take birth control or, I was sick all day. I had no morning sickness when I was pregnant. Because we were able to have children so easily, Ken's said, "If the Lord needs them to come that badly, then let them come."

When we first got married, we could have said we didn't want children "**YET**" because we couldn't afford them. We had $100.00 to our name, Ken was in school and, we only had one car the first 5 years of our marriage. When Ken was coaching and teaching school, we had an extra $30.00 a month spending money so again we could have said not "**YET**". When Ken decided to try "Real Estate", we really couldn't afford to have children but as we just let them come and did our best, by the time we had our 5th child we were building our "1st Perry Dream Home". We also started taking a fun, exotic vacation once a year. Number 6 child was 13 months later. And even though it was 5 years between the last two children we knew we were not finished until number 7 came. The number seven means COMPLETE or FINISHED. Our children have provided much of the motivation we needed to endure through hard things, and they helped us enjoy the good times. The proclamation says: "**Happiness in family life is most likely to be achieved when founded upon the teachings of the Lord Jesus Christ. Successful marriages and families are established and maintained on principles of faith, prayer, repentance, forgiveness, respect, love, compassion, work, and wholesome recreational activities.**"

ENDURING TO THE END
(The last part of the Doctrine of Christ)

Counsel from many church leaders, throughout our 52 years of marriage and my personal experiences through the "**5 Stages of Marriage**" taught by Laura Brotherson - makes sense to me. What I have learned, I want to pass on. I desire to share this information, to help our posterity gain a greater understanding of the gospel and of each stage of marriage, to help them **have the desire to navigate through these different stages, especially when they face struggles.** I have shared challenges, and testimony, to instill the truth that it takes consistent **faith, hope, and charity to endure.**

Hartman Rector said - to **Endure** in Charity is to:
1. Keep repenting - change our nature and change our heart.
2. Keep forgiving - Elder Holland – "The Ministry of Reconciliation". Oct 2018 on Healing and forgiveness. When we come to God for help – we must **FIRST reconcile with thy brother.**
3. Endure in charity - The Bible Dictionary says "**Charity is the highest, noblest, strongest kind of love, not merely affection**".

LOVE IS A "Conscious" CHOICE - Not a fleeting Emotion

Like practicing the piano, "**perfecting the act of love requires a lifetime of PRACTICE and good choices. The DAILY choices we make in our marriages and families are what shape lasting love.**" We come to see that as we actively try to **DO** things differently, Christ helps us to **BE** the people HE wants us to be—people like Him."5

We first increase our FAITH IN JESUS CHRIST, and we must have a DESIRE to, more fully develop these qualities in our lives.

"Christlike attributes are **GIFTS from God**, that come as we use our AGENCY righteously. Ask Heavenly Father to bless you with these attributes; YOU CANNOT DEVELOP OR ACQUIRE THEM WITHOUT HIS HELP." Our entire mortal experience is about progression, trying, failing, and trying again.

Elder Scott D. Whitting says, "**Be brave and ask your spouse what attribute of Christ you are in need of?**" **The development of spiritual strength is like acquiring physical strength**. A prayer for good health would be in vain if we weren't striving to achieve it through healthy eating, exercise, and sleeping habits. We cannot expect to reap where we have not sown. Similarly, we cannot expect a virtue without effort. Prayer by itself is insufficient. To access His grace, or divine help, He expects us to do everything in our power, to pray and act in faith." Jeffrey Marsh teaches:

"If you can, by faithfulness in this life, obtain the right to come up in the morning of the resurrection, you need entertain no fears that the wife will be dissatisfied with her husband, or the husband with the wife; for those of the 1st or Celestial Resurrection will be free from sin and from the consequences of sin."

"**Oneness in marriage is an ever-evolving journey of learning, growing, and experiencing—not a destination.** Peace, joy, pleasure, and mutual fulfillment of the deepest longs of the heart await those couples who are willing to **pay the price.** As we allow the **refiner's fire to transform our hear**t and soul, we can attain personal wholeness and eternal oneness in marriage, faithfully fulfilling our marital stewardship to each other and to God."1

Regular Temple Worship

"**In the Temple Sealing, couples are admonished to - CLEAVE to each other and COUNSEL together in love and righteousness {that means effectively communicate]. Temple marriage covenants do not magically bring equality, unity, and oneness to a partnership, but those covenants COMMIT us to a DEVELOPMENTAL PROCESS OF LEARNING AND GROWING TOGETHER BY PRACTICE. "**

Speaking from personal experience, I have a strong testimony and belief that regular Temple worship is the KEY or best thing Ken and I have done to create ONENESS and UNITY in our marriage. The most effective way for a couple to overcome any marital struggle is to spend time in the temple especially doing "Initiatory" and "Sealing's for ancestors". Listening to the blessings, promises, and counsel, over and over, helps put and keep things in their proper perspective.

I love the analogy Michael Wilcox uses; "Nobody Seals an Empty Jar" - p. 73. I have bottled a lot of fruit, and in order for the bottle to seal, and preserve the fruit for an extended time, the jar must be FULL of fruit. When we are sealed in the temple, it is as if the Lord hands us an empty jar and tell us to fill it with the fruits of a righteous marriage.

Blessings and promises of the temple are not automatic. **"OUR ABIDING (OR ENDURING) IN THE COVENANT ALLOWS THE LORD TO PLACE THE SEAL ON OUR COVENANT RELATIONSHIP AND PRESERVE IT FOR ETERNITY. ALL ORDINANCES, IN ORDER TO SECURE THE PROMISES, MUST BE PERFORMED BY PROPER AUTHORITY AND SEALED BY THE HOLY GHOST. THIS SEALING COMES WHEN COMPLIANCE WITH THE COVENANTS HAVE BEEN ACCOMPLISHED."**

In conclusion, I want to express gratitude to Ken for remaining my eternal companion throughout this ever-evolving earthly journey of learning, growing, and experiencing life together. Hopefully we can keep going and endure to the very end that we may enjoy Eternal Life with our Heavenly Father, Mother, and our Savior Jesus Christ. I am grateful we chose to endure through our power struggles and that we chose to build a conscious marriage. I'm glad we were willing to be awakened to our own imperfections and continue to try to TRANSFORM those things that make our life better together. I am grateful for all the positive influences, teachers, leaders, and those who have helped us develop the little **daily habits** that influence our **daily thoughts and feelings**. President Russell M. Nelson' said, "The promise of Life Everlasting does not mean simply to live for a really, really, really long time. . . .Eternal life is the kind and quality of life that Heavenly Father and His Beloved son Jesus Christ live.

One thing we have done, to help us be one is, **READ TOGETHER** as a couple. Some of my favorite books I would suggest are about the temple. They are:
- Michael Wilcox - Book - "House of Glory."
- Ed J. Pinegar - Book "The Temple - Gaining Knowledge and Power".
- Anthony Sweat - "The Holy Covenants"
- Kim Gibbs - "Understanding "The Sacred Symbolism of Temple Clothing". (This book is small, and I carry it in my temple bag so I can focus on one piece of clothing every week when I go to the temple.)

Even though I know I won't be able to finish this for all my grandchildren, let alone my great grandchildren - **To help bear my testimony of the Temple,** I started **three traditions:**

1. Prophets and other leaders have repeatedly taught the importance of having a **"Picture of the temple in every child's bedroom".** So, I made a Needlepoint picture to hang in each grandchild's bedroom when they turned 12 years old. This is to remind them that Jesus went to the temple when he was 12 years old.

Saint George Temple

2. An embroidered **Temple Apron** - when they went on a mission or got married in the temple.

TEMPLE APRON HISTORY
The first aprons used in the temple endowment
were made by Relief Society sisters
under the direction of the Prophet Joseph Smith.
Thereafter, aprons were often produced
by mothers and grandmothers
for their children and grandchildren.
Ceremonial clothing is now readily available, but
the TRADITION of making a handmade
HEIRLOOM APRON for family members
preserves the tie to our pioneer heritage.
With Much Love
Grandma Peggy

3. We have tried to make temple attendance a "Family Affair" as we have tried to plan regular **"COUSIN TEMPLE DAYS"**. We have attended many different temples and performed "Baptisms" for hundreds of our ancestors. In the Doctrine and Covenants 128:24 we are asked to offer unto the Lord an offering in righteousness; and present in His holy temple, A BOOK CONTAINING THE RECORDS OF OUR DEAD. For we without [our ancestors] cannot be made perfect; neither can they without us be made perfect. The "welding together" of our families across generations can occur only in the temples through the sealing ordinances.

Prophets and Apostles have promised the youth "protection against the intensifying influence of the adversary as they participate in and love this holy work".
Sister Becky Craven said: "The **MORE** we do to stay on the covenant path, the **MORE** our faith in Jesus Christ will grow. The **MORE** our faith grows, the **MORE** we desire to repent. The **MORE** we repent, the **MORE** we will strengthen our covenant relationship with God. That covenant relationship draws us to the **TEMPLE** because keeping temple covenants is how we endure to the end."

The Dyer Family Proclamation

by Ken

The Dyer family hereby proclaims at the behest of the Lord Jesus Christ, that God the Father and His Son Jesus Christ have created this universe and all the things that in it are. They are alive today and they govern the heavens and the earth. They govern with love and mercy over all their creations. Their work and their glory is to bring to pass the immortality and eternal life of man.

The sacrifice and atonement of Jesus Christ, our Savior, made it possible for every inhabitant that has ever lived on this earth to earn a degree of glory in the next life if they will keep the commandments of the true living God and repent of all their sins and transgressions.

The Lord Jesus Christ descended from His divinity to be a mortal here on earth, living the only perfect life so as to provide an infinite and eternal sacrifice and also a pattern for us to follow whereby we could attain a perfect happiness with our family in the Celestial Kingdom to live with and as our Eternal Father, Mother, and Savior Jesus Christ lives.

This promise and other covenants are made in the Temples of the Lord's church, the Church of Jesus Christ of Latter-Day Saints. It is the only church on the earth that contains the fulness of the gospel of Jesus Christ and the only church that has received the authority from God to provide our eternal salvation. These promises and covenants are for every nation, kindred, tongue, and people; the high and mighty or the lowly and meek. They are all the same to God.

Without vision we all perish. We testify that this vision is manifested by the continuing revelation that is received by the living prophet of the Church of Jesus Christ of Latter-Day Saints.

We bear testimony of these truths in the name of Jesus Christ Amen.

The Ken and Peggy Dyer Family

(D&C 124:2-11 – CFM - written 2021)

Ken and Peggy were looking for love,
Not expecting it on a blind date.
But affairs of the heart are not predictable,
Sometimes they even turn out first rate.

Maybe we started our relationship unsure,
Some might say we were even in a moat.
Soon our minds and hearts were touched,
Finding ourselves in the Lord's boat.

Thru the years, we've done our best,
To find the Lord and His Covenant Path.
To guide our posterity thru the storms of life,
To earn the Lord's reward and avoid His wrath.

We've loved our family and prayed for them,
Until we have found a few grey hairs.
Not expecting perfection, only progression,
In our heavenly home, "No Empty Chairs".

Gpa Ken

"No Empty Chairs"

Music by Janice Kapp Perry

Words by Orrin G. Hatch

1. Look around our family table
Every person in his place.
Memorize this happy moment
And each familiar face.

Look around our family circle,
Feel the love that we all share.
Life is sweet and so complete with
Each loved one **gathered** here.

There are no empty chairs at our table,
No empty feelings inside,
When all those we love are together
Here side by side.

2. Time will fly, and all to quickly
Some will leave to try their wings.
Empty places at our table
Will tug at our heart strings.

But the number at our table
Will increase as children come,
Bringing to our family table
Sweet innocence and fun.

We'll add a few more chairs to our table
A lot more laughter and love,
As our joy is multiplied daily
To fill our cup.

3. When there comes **a time for parting**
There will be no tears because
We will **set a grander table**
Where all may live in love.

There we'll **wait** for each dear loved one
Who will come to **take his place**
At the feast that lasts forever
In God's eternal place.

We'll have no empty chairs at our table
No empty feelings inside,
When all those we love are together
There, side by side.

May the circle not be broken,
May **each one return** to be
Safe within this peaceful haven
Through all eternity.

We'll have no empty chairs at our table
When all are **gathered above**,
No more empty chairs at our table
In heaven's home of love.

DYER FAMILY - Names and Number in the family

1. Ken
2. Peggy
3. Brandon
4. Tiffany Dyer Gordon
5. Travis
6. Brett
7. Brittany Dyer Anderson
8. Marc
9. Aaron
10. Scott Gordon
11. Kami Spiers
12. Shauntay Gordon Boardman
13. Alexis Gordon Dunford
14. Jayden
15. Jen Trujillo
16. Kylee
17. Treyson Gordon
18. Jeremy Anderson
19. Jaxson
20. Kendra Wimmer
21. Oakley Anderson
22. Jacob Gordon
23. Brickelle Dyer Keller
24. Hailey Anderson
25. Shaffer
26. Kaleb
27. Emily Parris
28. Xander Gordon
29. Cole
30. Ashton Anderson
31. Taytum
32. Kailor Gordon
33. Elle
34. Miles D.
35. Gabriel Gordon
36. Weston
37. Hayden Anderson
38. Alex Ovard
39. Stockton
40. Averi
41. Octavia Gordon
42. Logan
43. Penelope
44. Sloane Dyer
45. Grace Anderson
46. Sutton
47. Brigham Boardman
48. Andrew Dunford
49. Shayne
50. Jack Boardman
51. Owen
52. Benjamin Boardman
53. Dean Dunford
54. Miles Keller
55. Kamryn Contino
56. Drew Dunford
57. Cailee Smith
58. Zoe Isabelle Brusa
59. Nate Headrick
60. Maverick Boardman
61. Meg Elizabeth Larsen
62. (Trey & Zoe) Ozzy Wren
63. Miles/Brickelle Leila May
64. Allix Ann Gomez
65. Tayja Michelle Corpuz
66. Baby Headrick

Made in the USA
Las Vegas, NV
08 October 2022

56790221R00043